YOUR KNOWLEDGE HAS VALUE

Immanuel Haller

Perseverance of Salvation

Can faith be lost?

GRIN Verlag

Bibliografische Information der Deutschen Nationalbibliothek:

Die Deutsche Bibliothek verzeichnet diese Publikation in der Deutschen National-
bibliografie; detaillierte bibliografische Daten sind im Internet über http://dnb.d-
nb.de/ abrufbar.

Imprint:

Copyright © 2007 GRIN Verlag GmbH
Druck und Bindung: Books on Demand GmbH, Norderstedt Germany
ISBN: 978-3-656-23733-4

This book at GRIN:

http://www.grin.com/en/e-book/196317/perseverance-of-salvation

GRIN - Your knowledge has value

Der GRIN Verlag publiziert seit 1998 wissenschaftliche Arbeiten von Studenten, Hochschullehrern und anderen Akademikern als eBook und gedrucktes Buch. Die Verlagswebsite www.grin.com ist die ideale Plattform zur Veröffentlichung von Hausarbeiten, Abschlussarbeiten, wissenschaftlichen Aufsätzen, Dissertationen und Fachbüchern.

Visit us on the internet:

http://www.grin.com/

http://www.facebook.com/grincom

http://www.twitter.com/grin_com

CONTINENTAL THEOLOGICAL SEMINARY

PERSEVERANCE OF SALVATION –
CAN FAITH BE LOST?

An essay prepared
For the course:
Christology / Soteriology

by
Immanuel Haller

Brussels, Belgium
Semester 1, December 2007

TABLE OF CONTENTS

INTRODUCTION

While some would argue that "those who have true faith can lose their faith neither totally nor finally," others believe that faith can be lost even though you have been a true Christian.[1] This paper has the aim to compare Arminian and Calvinist traditions concerning the theology of perseverance of the believer and concluding with the writers' view about this subject.

The aspect of perseverance is just a little puzzle in the whole discussion between Calvinism and Arminianism which is linked with many aspects, especially the doctrine of election. The following paper is just focused on the main thought which brought the writer to the final conclusion that a real Christian can lose salvation. The limitation of words does not allow us to touch the aspects of adoption, or the practical aspects of how a Christian can lose salvation.

First of all, we get a brief overview about Calvinism and Arianism concerning the question of perseverance. Secondly, we look at the question of election and see how these aspects relate to perseverance. Thirdly, we touch the topic of salvation and see if perseverance is conditional or unconditional. Lastly, we notice the vital importance of having a balanced view between divine care and the responsibility of the believer.

---

[1] Anthony A. Hoekem, *Saved by Grace* (Grand Rapids, MI: Eerdmans, 1989), 234.

PERSEVERANCE OF SALVATION

Calvinist Tradition

Calvinists believe that God has elected in His sovereign will or good pleasure certain individuals out of fallen humanity to receive eternal life.[2] They believe that election is unconditional and does not depend upon human beings performing a specific action or meeting certain conditions or terms of God. In other words, those which God chose will necessarily come to receive eternal life, because His election is from all eternity and immutable.

In the same manner, they argue that if the elect could at some point lose their salvation, God's election of them to eternal life would not be truly effectual. Consequently, election as understood by the Calvinists requires perseverance as well. In conclusion, they believe that salvation can not be lost if God elected you.

---

[2] Millard J. Erikson, *Introducing Christian Doctrine,* ed.R. Arnold Hustad (Grand Rapids, MI: Backer Academic, 2005), 300.

Arminian Tradition

While statements of the Arminian view vary to some degree, their starting point is the concept that God desires all persons to be saved.[3] They point to some definite assertions of the scripture that the Lord does not want "that any should perish, but that all should reach repentance."[4] Moreover, they believe that God's grace is given by God to all persons indiscriminately. Arminians argue with regard to Romans 8:29 that those who are predestined by God are those who in his infinite knowledge, He is able to foresee that they will accept the offer of salvation made in Jesus Christ.[5]

Arminians affirm that all believers can have full assurance of salvation with the condition that they remain in Christ. But, because salvation is conditioned on faith, perseverance is also conditioned.[6] The theological term which is used here is Conditional Perservation of the Saints.

Consequently Arminians believe that Apostasy (turning from Christ) is possible but only committed through a deliberate, willful rejection of Jesus and renouncement of belief.[7] In other words, Arminians believe salvation can be lost.

---

[3] Samuel Wakefield, *A complete System of Christian Theology* (Cincinnati: Hitchcock & Walden, 1869), 387.
[4] 2 Peter 3:9
[5] Erickson, 301.
[6] Robert Picirilli, *Grace, Faith, Free Will: Contrasting Views of Salvation: Calvinism and Arminianism* (Nashville: Randall House Publications, 2002), 203.
[7] Ibid, 204.

Election

Predestination and human freedom

By looking at the question of predestination we first of all have to confess that with our human mind we will never fully comprehend. If there were not so many passages of scripture where we read about God's will for salvation for anyone, our disability to bring divine predestination and personal human freedom of decision to a common denominator, we would just as Calvin come to the conclusion of the double predestination.[8]

However, from the perspective of the parable of the marriage of the King's Son in Matthew 22, we see that the calling from God's side had to be accepted (in reversal, repentance and conversion) by humans. Who does not assume God's offer is not part of the chosen ones and he will fare like the man who can not stand up to the king without wedding dress (Matthew 22:12). Despite his appointment to the Kingdom of Heaven, he is lost. The Parable ends by telling us that: "many are called, but few are chosen," (Matthew 22.14). The writer agrees with Donald Guthrie's Conclusion, that the chosen ones are those which really have accepted the invitation.[9] On the other hand, he disagrees with Arminius that election is the result of a human act.[10]

---

[8] Erich Mauerhofer, *Course outline for Soteriologie*, Theologische Hochschule Basel, Basel 2007, 43.

[9] Donald Guthrie, *New Testament Theology* (Illinois: Inter- Varsity Press, 1981).

[10] Florian Sonderheimer, *Course outline Sot. 5-2*, Bucheggg Bibelschule, Zürich, 2006, 2.

Before knowledge of God

A comparison of all passages about election with all the passages that call to conversion shows that God's predestination does not take place independently of human decision.[11] See for example Revelation 13:8 and 3:5. To our limited, human understanding the fact of the "before knowledge"[12] or the "before seeing" equals the "providence of God" can easier be comprehended.[13]

As a last point about election, it is interesting to note, that the Bible calls believers the elected with their acceptance of salvation, and not before.[14] The following quote illustrates this truth: "You stand before the gate and read on the top of it 'Whosoever' then you walk through and look back and read on top of the gate 'Chosen'."[15]

The paper showed that the concept of election is always connected with human personal freedom of decision. God's election is never an edict. By looking at the question of perseverance we therefore disagree with the Calvinist concept that perseverance is the result of God's election.

---

[11] Mauerhofer, 43.

[12] Romans 8:29 (NKJV)

[13] Mauerhofer, 44.

[14] Mauerhofer, 45.

[15] Free Quote, Author unknown

Perseverance

Salvation

Before speaking about perseverance, we should not forget the facts in which Arminians and Calvinists at least in their usual forms agree. Salvation is neither attained or retained by works of the human person but by the saving work of Jesus Christ. Both are convinced that salvation is provided by God. They both insist that the believer can indeed know that he or she currently possesses salvation and that God is powerful, faithful, willing and able to keep His promises.

Calvinistic Bible support

We agree with the emphasis which Calvinists make saying that God does not simply give us eternal life and then abandon us to our human self-efforts. Rather, the work He began in us continues until it is completed (Philippians 1:6). Moreover, Christ constantly intercedes for us to the Father (Hebrew 7:25), who always hears His prayers (John 11:42). Furthermore, Calvinists highlight that because of God's provisions, we will be able to deal with and overcome whatever obstacles and temptations come our way. Our Master will enable His servants to stand in the face of judgement (Romans 14:4) and because of God's provision, we will be able to cope with temptation (1 Corinthians 10:13).

Arminian bible support

Eventhough the writer likes the Calvinist emphasis of God's providence there are numerous Biblical teaching which serve independently to support the doctrine of Conditional Perseverance of the Saints.

First of all, there are a number of warnings against apostasy. Jesus warned his disciples about the danger of being led astray.[16] Hebrews 2:1 says: "Therefore we we must give the more earnest heed to the things we have heard, lest we drift away." Or with Colossians 1:12: "…that you continue in the faith, stable and steadfast, not shifting from the

---

[16] Matthew 24.3-14

hope of the gospel which you heard." We agree with the Arminian view, saying that it is difficult to understand why such warnings were given if the believer cannot fall away.[17]

Secondly, we find clear statements about people who, having had the experience of salvation, depart from it. Judas betrayed Jesus and ended his life by not returnig to Christ. Ananias and Sapphira,[18] Hymenaus und Alexander, who "by rejecting consciense ... have made shipwreck of their faith."[19] Furthermore, Demas[20] and the false teachers and those who follow them in 2 Peter 2:1. With regard to Hebrew 6:4-8, 10:26-31 and 2 Peter 2:20-22, the writer can not follow the pattern of Calvinist argumentation that these were not real Christians.[21]

Thirdly, we agree with the Arminian objection that the Calvinistic view of perseverance is in conflict with the scriptural concept of human freedom. If it is certain that those who are in Christ will persevere and not fall away, then it must surely be the case that they are unable to choose apostasy. And if this is the case, they cannot be free. Yet Scripture, the Arminians point out, depicts humans as free beings, for they are repeatedly exhorted to choose God and are clearly portrayed as being held responsible by Him for their actions.[22]

Moltmann chracterises the difference between Arminian and Calvinist views of Perseverance accurately as follows: "While for the Arminiens God's arms remain open so that everybody can always return to Him, for the Calvinists God's arms have embraced the sinner and would not let him go."[23]

---

[17] Dale Moody, *The Word of Truth: A Summary of Christian Doctrine Based on Biblical Revelation* (Grand Rapids: Eerdmans, 1981), 350-54.

[18] Acts 5:1-11

[19] 1 Timothy 1:19-20

[20] 2 Timothy 4:10

[21] Jacob Thiessen, Biblische Glaubenslehre: *Eine Systematische Theologie für jedermann* (Plata, Paraguay: Verlag der Bibelschule Loma Plata, 2003), 169.

[22] Erikson, 331.

[23] J. Moltmann, Prädestination und Perseveranz (Neukirchen: Neukirchener Verlag, 1961) A brief survey of the history of the doctrine of perseverance is J.J Davis, 'The Perseverance of the Saints: A History of the Doctrine', in *Journal of the Evangelical Theological Society*, 34.2 (1991) 213.

Divine grace and the believers responsibility

There are passages from the Bible about the topic of perseverance which seem to contradict at a superficial consideration. For example:

> John 10:27-28: "My sheep hear my voice, and I know them, and they follow me. And I give them eternal live, and they shall never perish, neither shall anyone snatch them out of my hand."

> John 15:2-6: "Every branch in Me that does not bear fruit He takes away, and every branch that bears fruit he prunes, that it may bear more fruit… "If anyone does not abide in Me, he is cast out as a branch and is withered; and they gather them into the fire, and they are burned."

The apparent problem can only be solved taking into account the tension between encouragement and comfort and admonishment on the other side. While Calvinism highlights the divine care Arminanism highlights the responsibility of the believer. Or in other words, the Arminian view ascribes altogether too much the will of man, despite the guarded nature of its affirmation, and the Calvinist view ascribes everything ultimately to the irresistible grace of God.[24] Emphasising the former would lead to spiritual complacency or introspection and emphasising the later would lead to spiritual legalism.[25]

However, from our understanding of scripture, the believer is not told that he can not fall away. The believer is simply told to continue in obedience and faith, and to trust in the God who will keep him from falling. He perseveres by persevering.[26] Perseverance is therefore not some particular quality of faith, or something to be added to faith, but the fact that faith continues.[27]

A balanced view between the emphasis of divine care and the responsibility of the believer is therefore important. Paul expresses the tension of that issue in challenging us to "work out your own salvation with fear and trembling" in awareness that "God is it who works in you both to will and to do for His good pleasure."[28]

---

[24] Howard Marshall, *Kept by the Power of God: A Study of Perseverance and Falling Away* (Carlistle: Paternoster Press, 1995), 208.
[25] Jan Henzel, "And Grace will lead me home: perseverance of believers as divine gift and human responsibility." European Journal of Theology (12 no 1 2003): 32.
[26] Marshall, 208.
[27] Ibid.
[28] Philippians 2:12-13

CONCLUSION

The writer showed that the concept of election is always to see in connection with personal human freedom of decision, and that God's election is never an edict. Rejecting the doctrine of unconditional election, he consequently rejects the doctrine of final perseverance. We saw the many warnings in the scripture not to fall away from the faith, and the tragical examples which fell away from faith.

In conclusion, the writer agrees with the doctrine of Wesley about the conditional perseverance of faith, which shows the earnest fact that a Christian can be lost. Having said this, however, we must note that the right balance in the tension between divine gift and the responsibility of the believer shows that the Armenian and the Calvinistic positions highlight both a part truth.

BIBLIOGRAPHY

Arthur, Mac., and John F. "Perseverance of the saints" *Master's Seminary Journal* (4 no 1 spring 1993): 5-24.

Erikson, Millard. *Introducing Christian Doctrine*. Grand Rapids, MI: Backer Academic, 2005.

Finney, Charles. *Lebenserinnerungen*. Giessen, DE: Brunnen, 1965

Henzel, Jan. "And Grace will lead me home: perseverance of believers as divine gift and human responsibility." *European Journal of Theology* (12 no 1 2003): 27-34.

Hoekema, Anthony. *Saved by Grace*. Grand Rapids: MI Eerdmans, 1989.

Marshall, Howard. *Kept by the Power of God*: A Study of Perseverance and Falling Away. Carlistle: Paternoster Press, 1995.

Mauerhofer, Erich. *Course outline Soteriologie*, Theologische Hochschule Basel, 2007.

Moody, Dale. *The Word of Truth: A Summary of Christian Doctrine Based on Biblical Revelation*. Grand Rapids: Eerdmans, 1981.

Peters, Benedikt. *George Whitefield: Der Erwecker Englands und Amerikas*. Bielefeld, DE: CLV, 1997.

Picirilli, Robert. *Grace, Faith, Free Will: Contrasting Views of Savation: Calvinism and Arminianism*. Nashville, TN: Randall House Publications, 2002.

Sonderheimer, Florian. *Course outline* Sot. 5-2, Buchegg Bibelschule, Zürich, 2006.

Thiessen, Jacob. *Biblische Glaubenslehre: Eine Systematische Theologie für jedermann*. Plata, Paraguay: Verlag der Bibelschule Loma Plata, 2003.

Wakefield, Samuel. *A complete System of Christian Theology*. Cincinnati: Hitchcock & Walden, 1869.

Wilder-Smith, Arthur E. *Ist das ein Gott der Liebe*. Neuhausen, DE: Hänssler, 1988.